RENDEZVOUS WITH DESTINY

RENDEZVOUS WITH DESTINY

By President
RONALD REAGAN

OSMOND PUBLISHING COMPANY
Salt Lake City

Published by
OSMOND PUBLISHING COMPANY
1816 Grover Lane
Salt Lake City, Utah 84117

Printed and bound in the United States
of America.

First Printing

Designed by Ronald Crosby

LIBRARY OF CONGRESS CATALOG CARD NO. 81-38339
ISBN 0-89888-026-2

TRIBUTE
By
Charlton Heston
at the Gala prior to the Inauguration
of
Ronald Reagan

Tomorrow at high noon on the west front of the Capitol, there will occur an event almost unique in the world. Without force, or coercion, with neither the threat of military violence nor parliamentary abrasion, one man will peacefully transfer to another the most awesome power and influence ever put in the hand of a single human being.

The man who holds this power will pass it on in civil and congenial obedience to the custom of two centuries.

The man who receives it will inherit more than just a constitutional legacy. He will be forever wrapped in legend and myth. He will also lift tomorrow a burden of responsibility that has no known counterpart in the civilized world.

American writers have been exploring this country and its people throughout our history.

William Faulkner, accepting the Nobel Prize in 1950, said:

"I decline to accept the end of man. It is easy enough to say that man is immortal simply because he will endure: that when the last ding dong of doom has clanged and faded from the last worthless rock hanging tideless in the last red and dying evening, that even then there will still be one more sound; that of his puny, inexhaustible voice, still talking. I refuse to accept this. I believe that man will not merely endure, he will prevail. He is immortal, not because he alone among creatures has an

5

inexhaustible voice, but because he has a soul, a spirit capable of compassion, and sacrifice, and endurance."

The great historian, Samuel Eliot Morison, wrote with equal eloquence of the way this country confronts history. He said:

"Americans have always taken themselves and their democracy for granted: in a land of opportunity, we have been opportunists. The current of our national life has been so swift as to develop that sort of quick thinking and instinctive action a good raftsman uses to avoid the rocks as he shoots the white water. Now we've passed the rapids of our river, into the level reaches that lead to the mysterious ocean of the future. For that deep-sea voyage we'll need expert seamen; clear-thinking, courageous, with the wisdom that comes of experience: The experience of our sister ships as well as our own. To develop these qualities we need not break with our past. On the contrary, we'll *need* all of the blithe fearlessness, the kindliness and simplicity, the passionate yearning for righteousness, that has redeemed our past. To fulfill the bright promise of her birth, America must grow out of her youth slowly, and never quite outgrow it. She must be linked not only to the forms and institutions of her past, but to its living, fruitful spirit."

F. Scott Fitzgerald defined the unique quality in the American character as "...a willingness of the heart." But Thomas Wolfe, in his novel "OF TIME AND THE RIVER", used a poet's instincts to capture the American fabric...our country and our people.

"It is a fabulous country, the only fabulous country; it's the one place where miracles not only happen, but where they happen all the time.

It's the place of exultancy and strong joy, the place of the darkened brooding air, the smell of snow; the place of all the fierce, the bitten colors in October, when all of the wild, sweet woods flame up. The place of the cider press and the last brown oozings of the York Imperials.

It's the place where great boats are baying at the harbor's mouth, where great ships are putting out to sea; great boats blowing in the gulf of night, and where the river, the dark and secret river, full of strange time, is forever flowing by us to the sea.

It's the place of autumnal moons hung low and orange at the frosty edges of the pines; the place of frost and silence; of the clean dry shocks and the opulence of enormous pumpkins that yellow on hard clotted earth. It's the place of the stir and feathery stumble of the hens upon their roost, the frosty, broken barking of the dogs, the great barn-shapes and solid shadows in the running sweep of the moon-whited countryside, the wailing whistle of the fast express.

It's the place of the wild and exultant winter's morning where the wind, with the powdery snow, has been howling all night long in solitude and the branches of the spruce and hemlock are piled with snow. It's the place where the fall river boats are tethered to the wharf, and the wild gray snow of furious, secret, and storm-whited morning whips across them. It is the place of the lodge by the frozen lake and the sweet breath and amorous flesh of woman; it is the place of the tragic and lonely beauty of New England...the red barn, and the sound of the stabled hooves, and the bright tatters of old circus posters. It's the place of the immense and pungent smell of breakfast: the country sausages and the ham and eggs, the smoking wheat cakes and the fragrant coffee, and of lone hunters in the frosty thickets, who whistle to their lop-eared hounds.

It is the immense, and lonely, and abundant land, where they grow cotton, corn, and wheat, and the wine-red apples of October.

It is the place that is savage and cruel, but it is also the innocent place; it is the wild, lawless place, the vital earth that is soaked with the blood of the countless murdered men, with the blood of the unavenged and unremembered murdered men; but it is also the place of the child and laughter, where the young men are torn apart with ecstasy, and cry out in their throats with joy, where they hear the howl of the wind and the rain and smell the thunder and the soft numb spitting of the snow, where they are drunk with the bite and sparkle of the air and mad with the solar energy, where they believe in love and victory and think that we can never die."

In a few hours Ronald Reagan will become the lineal descendant of Washington and Adams, Jefferson and Jackson, Lincoln, Wilson, Roosevelt. With them, he will be linked to the very birth year of this Republic.

The President. What do we pray for him? What do we wish from him and for him? What can he pledge to us? What can we say to help him?

Perhaps the answers lie in who we are, and where we are. Yes, God bless Ronald Reagan.

"A TIME FOR CHOOSING"
NATIONAL TELEVISION SPEECH
DELIVERED OCTOBER 1964
BY RONALD REAGAN

In October, nineteen sixty-four, a fifty-three year old Ronald Reagan delivered a masterful speech over national television. Its impact on the American public was so great, that he was urged to run for the Governorship of California. After much deliberation, he accepted the challenge, and won the election over the incumbent by over one million votes. Here is the speech that started the political career of Ronald Reagan.

I am going to talk of controversial things. I make no apology for this. I have been talking on this subject for ten years obviously under the administration of both parties. I mention this only because it seems impossible to legitimately debate the issues of the day without being subjected to name-calling and the application of labels. Those who deplore use of the terms "pink" and "leftist" are themselves guilty of branding all who oppose their liberalism as right wing extremists. How long can we afford the luxury of this family fight when we are at war with the most dangerous enemy ever known to man?

If we lose that war, and in so doing lose our freedom, it has been said history will record with the greatest astonishment that those who had the most to lose did the least to prevent its happening. The guns are silent in this war but frontiers fall while those who should be warriors prefer neutrality. Not too long ago two friends of mine were talking to a Cuban refugee.

He was a business man who had escaped from Castro. In the midst of his tale of horrible experiences, one of my friends turned to the other and said, "We don't know how lucky we are." The Cuban stopped and said, "How lucky you are? I had some place to escape to." And in that sentence he told the entire story. If freedom is lost here there is no place to escape to.

It's time we asked ourselves if we still know the freedoms intended for us by the Founding Fathers. James Madison said, "We base all our experiments on the capacity of mankind for self-government." This idea that government was beholden to the people, that it had no other source of power except the sovereign people, is still the newest, most unique idea in all the long history of man's relation to man. For almost two centuries we have proved man's capacity for self-government, but today we are told we must choose between a left and right or, as others suggest, a third alternative, a kind of safe middle ground. I suggest to you there is no left or right, only an up or down. Up to the maximum of individual freedom consistent with law and order, or down to the ant heap of totalitarianism, and regardless of their humanitarian purpose those who would sacrifice freedom for security have, whether they know it or not, chosen this downward path. Plutarch warned, "The real destroyer of the liberties of the people is he who spreads among them bounties, donations and benefits."

Today there is an increasing number who can't see a fat man standing beside a thin one without automatically coming to the conclusion the fat man got that way by taking advantage of the thin one. So they would seek the answer to all the problems of human need through government. Howard K. Smith of television fame has written, "The profit motive is outmoded. It must be replaced by incentives of the welfare state." He says, "The distribution of goods must be effected by a planned economy."

Another articulate spokesman for the welfare state defines liberalism as meeting the material needs of the masses through the full power of centralized government. I for one find it disturbing when a representative refers to the free men and women of this country as the masses, but beyond this the full power of centralized government was the very thing the Founding Fathers sought to minimize. They knew you don't control things, you can't control the economy without controlling people. So we have come to a time for choosing. Either we accept the responsibility for our own destiny, or we abandon the American Revolution and confess that an intellectual belief in a far-distant capitol can plan our lives for us better than we can plan them ourselves.

Already the hour is later. Government has laid its hand on health, housing, farming, industry, commerce, education, and to an ever-increasing degree interferes with the people's right to know. Government tends to grow, government programs take on weight and momentum as public servants say, always with the best of intentions, "What greater service we could render if only we had a little more money and a little more power." But the truth is that outside of its legitimate function, government does nothing as well or economically as the private sector of the economy. What better example do we have of this than government's involvement in the farm economy over the last 30 years. One-fourth of farming has seen a steady decline in the per capita consumption of everything it produces. That one-fourth is regulated and subsidized by government.

In contrast, the three-fourths of farming unregulated and

11

unsubsidized has seen a 21 per cent increase in the per capita consumption of all its produce. Since 1955 the cost of the farm program has nearly doubled. Direct payment to farmer is eight times as great as it was nine years ago, but farm income remains unchanged while farm surplus is bigger. In that same period we have seen a decline of five million in the farm population, but an increase in the number of Department of Agriculture employees.

There is now one such employee for every 30 farms in the United States, and still they can't figure how 66 shiploads of grain headed for Austria could disappear without a trace, and Billy Sol Estes never left shore. Three years ago the government put into effect a program to curb the over-production of feed grain. Now, two and a half billion dollars later, the corn crop is 100 million bushels bigger than before the program started. And the cost of the program prorates out to $43 for every dollar bushel of corn we don't grow. Nor is this the only example of the price we pay for government meddling. Some government programs with the passage of time take on a sacrosanct quality.

One such considered above criticism, sacred as motherhood is TVA. This program started as a flood control project: The Tennessee Valley was periodically ravaged by destructive floods. The Army Engineers set out to solve this problem. They said that it was possible that once in 500 years there could be a total capacity flood that would inundate some 600,000 acres. Well the Engineers fixed that. They made a permanent lake which inundated a million acres. This solved the problem of the floods, but the annual interest on the TVA debt is five times as great as the annual flood damage they sought to correct.

Of course, you will point out that TVA gets electric power from the impounded waters, and this is true, but today 85 per cent of TVA's electricity is generated in coal burning steam plants. Now perhaps you'll charge that I'm overlooking the navigable waterway that was created, providing cheap barge traffic, but the bulk of the freight barged on that waterway is coal being shipped to the TVA steam plants, and the cost of maintaining that channel each year would pay for shipping all of the coal by rail, and there would be money left over.

One last argument remains. The prosperity produced by such large programs of government spending. Certainly there are few areas where more spending has taken place. The Labor Department lists 50 per cent of the 169 counties in the Tennessee Valley as permanent areas of poverty, distress, and unemployment.

Meanwhile, back in the city, under Urban Renewal, the assault on freedom carries on. Private property rights have become so diluted that public interest is anything a few planners decide it should be. In Cleveland, Ohio, to get a project under way, city officials reclassified 84 buildings as substandard in spite of the fact their own inspectors had previously pronounced these buildings sound. The owners stood by and watched 26 million dollars worth of property as it was destroyed by the headache ball. Senate Bill 628 says, "Any property, be it home or commercial structure, can be declared slum or blighted and the owner has no recourse at law. The Law Division of the Library of Congress and the General Accounting Office have said that the Courts will have to rule against the owner."

HOUSING. In one key Eastern city a man owning a blighted area sold his property to Urban Renewal for several million dollars. At the same time, he submitted his own plan for the rebuilding of this area and the government sold him back his own property for 22 per cent of what they paid. Now the government announces, "We are going to build subsidized housing in the thousands where we have been building in the hundreds." At the same time FHA and the Veterans Administration reveal they are holding 120 thousand housing units reclaimed from mortgage foreclosure, mostly because the low down payment, and the easy terms brought the owners to a point where they realized the unpaid balance on the homes amounted to a sum greater than the homes were worth, so they just walked out the front door, possibly to take up residence in newer subsidized housing, again with little or no down payment and easy terms.

Some of the foreclosed homes have already been bulldozed into the earth, others, it has been announced, will be refurbished and put on sale for down payments as low as $100 and 35 years to pay. This will give the bulldozers a second crack. It is in the area of social welfare that government has found its most fertile growing bed. So many of us accept our responsibility for those less fortunate. We are susceptible to humanitarian appeals.

Federal welfare spending is today ten times greater than it was in the dark depths of the depression. Federal, state, and local welfare combined spend 45 billion dollars a year. Now the government has announced that 20 per cent, some 9.3 million families, are poverty stricken on the basis that they have less than a $3,000 a year income.

If this present welfare spending was prorated equally among these poverty stricken families, we could give each family more than $4,500 a year. Actually, direct aid to the poor averages less than $600 per family. There must be some administrative overhead somewhere. Now, are we to believe that another billion dollar program added to the half a hundred programs and the 45 billion dollars, will, through some magic, end poverty? For three decades we have tried to solve unemployment by government planning, without success. The more the plans fail, the more the planners plan.

The latest is the Area Redevelopment Agency, and in two years less than one-half of one per cent of the unemployed could attribute new jobs to this agency, and the cost to the taxpayer for each job found was $5,000. But beyond the great bureaucratic waste, what are we doing to the people we seek to help?

Recently a judge told me of an incident in his court. A fairly young woman with six children, pregnant with her seventh, came to him for a divorce. Under his questioning it became apparent her husband did not share this desire. Then the whole story came out. Her husband was a laborer earning $250 a month. By divorcing him she could get an $80 raise. She was eligible for $350 a month from the Aid to Dependent Children Program. She had been talked into the divorce by two friends who had already done this very thing. But any time we question the schemes of the do-gooders, we are denounced as being opposed to their humanitarian goal. It seems impossible to legitimately debate their solutions with the assumption that all of us share the desire to help those less fortunate. They tell us we are always against, never for anything. Well, it isn't so much that Liberals are ignorant. It's just that they know so much that isn't so.

We are for a provision that destitution should not follow unemployment by reason of old age. For that reason we have accepted Social Security as a step toward meeting that problem. However, we are against the irresponsibility of those who charge that any criticism or suggested improvement of the program means we want to end payment to those who depend on Social Security for livelihood.

FISCAL IRRESPONSIBILITY. We have been told in millions of pieces of literature and press releases that Social Security is an insurance program, but the executives of Social Security appeared before the Supreme Court in the case of Nestor v. Fleming and proved to the Court's satisfaction that it is not insurance but is a welfare program, and Social Security is today 209 billion dollars in the red. This fiscal irresponsibility has already caught up with us.

Faced with a bankruptcy we find that today a young man in his early twenties, going to work at less than an average salary, will with his employer pay into Social Security an amount which could provide the young man with a retirement insurance policy guaranteeing $220 a month at age 65, and the government promises him $127.

Now, are we so lacking in business sense that we cannot put this program on a sound actuarial basis, so that those who do depend on it won't come to the cupboard and find it bare, and at the same time can't we introduce voluntary features so that those who can make better provision for themselves are allowed to do so? Incidentally, we might also allow participants in Social Security to name their own beneficiaries, which they cannot do in the present program. These are not insurmountable problems.

YOUTH AID PLANS. We have today 30 million workers protected by industrial and union pension funds that are soundly financed by some 70 billion dollars invested in corporate securities and income-earning real estate. I think we are for telling our senior citizens that no one in this country should be denied medical care for lack of funds but we are against forcing all citizens into a compulsory government program regardless of need. Now the government has turned its attention to our young people, and suggests that it can solve the problem of school dropouts and juvenile delinquency through some kind of revival of the old C.C.C. camps. The suggested plan prorates out to a cost of $4,700 a year for each young person we want to help. We can send them to Harvard for $2,700 a year. Of course, don't get me wrong—I'm not suggesting Harvard as the answer to juvenile delinquency.

We are for an international organization where the nations of the world can legitimately seek peace. We are against subordinating American interests to an organization so structurally unsound that a two-thirds majority can be mustered in the U.N. General Assembly among nations representing less than 10 per cent of the world population.

Is there not something of hypocrisy in assailing our allies for so-called vestiges of colonialism while we engage in a conspiracy of silence about the peoples enslaved by the Soviet in the satellite nations? We are for aiding our allies by sharing our material blessings with those nations which share our fundamental beliefs. We are against doling out money, government to government, which ends up financing socialism all over the world.

We set out to help 19 war ravaged countries at the end of World War II. We are now helping 107. We have spent 146 billion dollars. Some of that money bought a $2 million yacht for Haile Selassie. We bought dress suits for Greek undertakers. We bought 1,000 TV sets, with 23-inch screens, for a country where there is no electricity, and some of our foreign aid funds provided extra wives for Kenya government officials. When Congress moved to cut foreign aid they were told that if they cut it one dollar they endangered national security, and then Senator Harry Byrd revealed that since its inception foreign aid has rarely spent its allotted budget. It has today $21 billion in unexpended funds.

Sometime ago Dr. Howard Kershner was speaking to the prime minister of Lebanon. The prime minister told him proudly that his little country balanced its budget each year. It had no public debt, no inflation, a modest tax rate and had increased its gold holdings from 70 to 120 million dollars. When he finished, Dr. Kershner said, "Mr. Prime Minister, my country hasn't balanced its budget 28 out of the last 40 years. My country's debt is greater than the combined debt of all the nations of the world. We have inflation, we have a tax rate that takes from the private sector a percentage of income greater than any civilized nation has ever taken and survived. We have lost gold at such a rate that the solvency of our currency is in danger. Do you think that my country should continue to give your country millions of dollars each year?" The prime minister smiled and said, "No, but if you are foolish enough to do it, we are going to keep on taking the money."

9 STALLS FOR 1 BULL. And so we built a model stock farm in Lebanon, and we built nine stalls for each bull. I find something peculiarly appropriate in that. We have in our vaults $15 billion in gold. We don't own an ounce. Foreign dollar claims against that gold total $27 billion. In the last six years, 52 nations have bought $7 billion worth of our gold and all 52 are receiving foreign aid.

Because no government ever voluntarily reduces itself in

size, government programs once launched never go out of existence. A government agency is the nearest thing to eternal life we'll ever see on this earth. The United States Manual takes 25 pages to list by name every Congressman and Senator, and all the agencies controlled by Congress. It then lists the agencies coming under the Executive Branch, and this requires 520 pages.

Since the beginning of the century our gross national product has increased by 33 times. In the same period the cost of Federal government has increased 234 times, and while the work force is only 1½ times greater, Federal employees number nine times as many. There are now 2½ million Federal employees. No one knows what they all do. One Congressman found out what one of them does. This man sits at a desk in Washington. Documents come to him each morning. He reads them, initials them and passes them on to the proper agency. One day a document arrived he wasn't supposed to read, but he read it, initialled it and passed it on. Twenty-four hours later it arrived back at his desk with a memo attached that said, "You weren't supposed to read this. Erase your initials, and initial the erasure."

While the Federal government is the great offender, the idea filters down. During a period in California when our population has increased 90 per cent, the cost of state government has gone up 862 per cent and the number of employees 500 per cent. Governments, state and local, now employ one out of six of the nation's work force. If the rate of increase of the last three years continues, by 1970 one-fourth of the total work force will be employed by government. Already we have a permanent structure so big and complex it is virtually beyond the control of Congress and the comprehension of the people, and tyranny inevitably follows when this permanent structure usurps the policy-making function that belongs to elected officials.

One example of this occurred when Congress was debating whether to lend the United Nations $100 million. While they debated the State Department gave the United Nations $217 million and the United Nations used part of that money to pay the delinquent dues of Castro's Cuba.

Under bureaucratic regulations adopted with no regard to the wish of the people, we have lost much of our Constitutional freedom. For example, federal agents can invade a man's property without a warrant, can impose a fine without a formal hearing, let alone a trial by jury, and can seize and sell his property at auction to enforce payment of that fine.

RIGHTS BY DISPENSATION. An Ohio deputy fire marshal sentenced a man to prison after a secret proceeding in which the accused was not allowed to have a lawyer present. The Supreme Court upheld that sentence, ruling that it was an administrative investigation of incidents damaging to the economy. Someplace a perversion has taken place. Our natural unalienable rights are now presumed to be a dispensation of government, divisible by a vote of the majority. The greatest good for the greatest number is a high-sounding phrase but contrary to the very basis of our Nation, unless it is accompanied by recognition that we have certain rights which cannot be infringed upon, even if the individual stands outvoted by all of his fellow citizens. Without this recognition, majority rule is nothing more than mob rule.

It is time we realized that socialism can come without overt seizure of property or nationalization of private business. It matters little that you hold the title to your property or business if government can dictate policy and procedure and holds life and death power over your business. The machinery of this power already exists. Lowell Mason, former anti-trust law enforcer for the Federal Trade Commission, has written "American business is being harassed, bled and even black-jacked under a preposterous crazy quilt system of laws." There are so many that the government literally can find some charge to bring against any concern it chooses to prose-cute. Are we safe in our books and records?

The natural gas producers have just been handed a 428-page questionnaire by the Federal Power Commission. It weighs ten pounds. One firm has estimated it will take 70,000 accountant man hours to fill out this questionnaire, and it must be done in quadruplicate. The Power Commission says it must have it to determine whether a proper price is being charged for gas. The National Labor Relations Board ruled that a business firm could not discontinue its shipping depart-ment even though it was more efficient and economical to sub-contract this work out.

The Supreme Court has ruled the government has the right to tell a citizen what he can grow on his own land for his own use. The Secretary of Agriculture has asked for the right to imprison farmers who violate their planting quotas. One business firm has been informed by the Internal Revenue Service that it cannot take a tax deduction for its institutional advertising because this advertising espoused views not in the public interest.

A child's prayer in a school cafeteria endangers religious freedom but the people of the Amish religion in the State of Ohio who cannot participate in Social Security because of their religious beliefs have had their livestock seized and sold at auction to enforce payment of Social Security dues.

We approach a point of no return when government becomes so huge and entrenched that we fear the consequences of upheaval and just go along with it. The Federal government accounts for one-fifth of the industrial capacity of the nation, one-fourth of all construction, holds or guarantees one-third of all mortgages, owns one-third of the land, and engages in some nineteen thousand businesses covering half a hundred different lines. The Defense Department runs 269 supermarkets. They do a gross business of $730 million a year, and lose $150 million. The government spends $11 million an hour every hour of the 24 and pretends we had a tax cut while it pursues a policy of planned inflation that will more than wipe out any benefit with depreciation of our purchasing power.

We need true tax reform that will at least make a start toward restoring for our children the American dream that wealth is denied to no one, that each individual has the right to fly as high as his strength and ability will take him. The economist Sumner Schlicter has said, "If a visitor from Mars looked at our tax policy, he would conclude it had been designed by a Communist spy to make free enterprise unworkable." But we cannot have such reform while our tax policy is engineered by people who view the tax as a means of achieving changes in our social structure. Senator Clark (D.-Pa.) says the tax issue is a class issue, and the government must use the tax to redistribute the wealth and earnings downward.

KARL MARX. On January 15th in the White House, the President told a group of citizens they were going to take all the money they thought was being unnecessarily spent, "take it from the have's and give it to the have-nots who need it so much." When Karl Marx said this he put it: ....from each according to his ability to each according to his need."

Have we the courage and the will to face up to the immorality and discrimination of the progressive surtax, and demand a return to traditional proportionate taxation? Many decades ago the Scottish economist, John Ramsey McCulloch, said, "The moment you abandon the cardinal principle of exacting from all individuals the same proportion of their income or their property, you are at sea without a rudder or compass and there is no amount of injustice or folly you may not commit." No nation has survived the tax burden that reached one-third of its national income.

Today in our country the tax collector's share is 37 cents of every dollar earned. Freedom has never been so fragile, so close to slipping from our grasp. I wish I could give you some magic formula, but each of us must find his own role. One man in Virginia found what he could do, and dozens of business firms have followed his lead. Concerned because his 200 employees seemed unworried about government extravagance he conceived the idea of taking all of their withholding out of only the fourth paycheck, each month. For three paydays his employees received their full salary. On the fourth payday all withholding was taken. He has one employee who owes him $4.70 each fourth payday. It only took one month to produce 200 conservatives.

Are you willing to spend time studying the issues, making yourself aware, and then conveying that information to family and friends? Will you resist the temptation to get a government handout for your community? Realize that the doctor's fight against socialized medicine is your fight. We can't socialize the doctors without socializing the patients. Recognize that government invasion of public power is eventually an assault upon your own business...If some among you fear taking a stand because you are afraid of reprisals from customers, clients, or even government, recognize that you are just feeding the crocodile hoping he'll eat you last.

If all of this seems like a great deal of trouble think what's at stake. We are faced with the most evil enemy mankind has known in his long climb from the swamp to the stars. There can be no security anywhere in the free world if there is not fiscal and economic stability within the United States. Those who ask us to trade our freedom for the soup kitchen of the welfare state are architects of a policy of accommodation. They tell us that by avoiding a direct confrontation with the enemy he will learn to love us and give up his evil ways. All who oppose this idea are blanket indicted as war-mongers. Well let us set one thing straight, there is no argument with regard to peace and war. It is cheap demagoguery to suggest that anyone would want to send other people's sons to war. The only argument is with regard to the best way to avoid war. There is only one sure way—surrender.

APPEASEMENT OR COURAGE? The spectre our well meaning liberal friends refuse to face is that their policy of accommodation is appeasement, and appeasement does not give you a choice between peace and war, only between fight or surrender. We are told that the problem is too complex for a simple answer. They are wrong. There is no easy answer, but there is a simple answer. We must have the courage to do what we know is morally right, and this policy of accommodation asks us to accept the greatest possible immorality. We are being asked to buy our safety from the threat of the Bomb by selling into permanent slavery our fellow human beings

24

enslaved behind the iron curtain, to tell them to give up their hope of freedom because we are ready to make a deal with their slave masters.

Alexander Hamilton warned us that a ndation which can prefer disgrace to danger is prepared for a master and deserves one. Admittedly there is a risk in any course we follow. Choosing the high road cannot eliminate that risk. Already some of the architects of accommodation have hinted what their decision will be if their plan fails and we are faced with the final ultimatum. The English commentator Tynan has put it, "He would rather live on his knees than die on his feet." Some of our own have said "Better Red than dead." If we are to believe that nothing is worth the dying, when did this begin? Should Moses have told the children of Israel to live in slavery rather than dare the wilderness? Should Christ have refused the Cross? Should the patriots at Concord Bridge have refused to fire the shot heard round the world? Are we to believe that all the martyrs of history died in vain?

You and I have a rendezvous with destiny. We can preserve for our children this last best hope of man on earth or we can sentence them to take the first step into a thousand years of darkness. If we fail, at least let our children and our children's children say of us we justified our brief moment here. We did all that could be done.

INAUGURAL ADDRESS
OF PRESIDENT RONALD REAGAN
12:00 NOON EST
JANUARY 20, 1981

The date was Nov. 4, 1980. The pollsters said, "The race for the Presidency was too close to call." However, just prior to the election, a debate between President Jimmy Carter and Ronald Reagan took place, and the "undecided" became "decided"; Reagan was rewarded with a landslide victory.

After taking the oath of office, President Reagan delivered this inaugural address.

THE PRESIDENT: Senator Hatfield, Mr. Chief Justice, Mr. President, Vice President Bush, Vice President Mondale, Senator Baker, Speaker O'Neill, Reverend Moomaw, and my fellow citizens: To a few of us here today this is a solemn and most momentous occasion. And, yet, in the history of our nation it is a commonplace occurrence.

The orderly transfer of authority as called for in the Constitution routinely takes place, as it has for almost two centuries, and few of us stop to think how unique we really are. In the eyes of many in the world, this every-four-year ceremony we accept as normal is nothing less than a miracle.

Mr. President, I want our fellow citizens to know how much you did to carry on this tradition. By your gracious cooperation in the transition process you have shown a watch-

27

ing world that we are a united people pledged to maintaining a political system which guarantees individual liberty to a greater degree than any other, and I thank you and your people for all your help in maintaining the continuity which is the bulwark of our Republic. (Applause.)

The business of our nation goes forward. These United States are confronted with an economic affliction of great proportions. We suffer from the longest and one of the worst sustained inflations in our national history. It distorts our economic decisions, penalizes thrift and crushes the struggling young and the fixed-income elderly alike. It threatens to shatter the lives of millions of our people.

Idle industries have cast workers into unemployment, human misery, and personal indignity. Those who do work are denied a fair return for their labor by a tax system which penalizes successful achievement and keeps us from maintaining full productivity.

But great as our tax burden is, it has not kept pace with public spending. For decades we have piled deficit upon deficit, mortgaging our future and our children's future for the temporary convenience of the present. To continue this long trend is to guarantee tremendous social, cultural, political, and economic upheavals.

You and I, as individuals, can, by borrowing, live beyond our means, but for only a limited period of time. Why, then, should we think that collectively, as a nation, we're not bound by that same limitation?

We must act today in order to preserve tomorrow. And let there be no misunderstanding—we are going to begin to act beginning today.

The economic ills we suffer have come upon us over several

decades. They will not go away in days, weeks, or months, but they will go away. They will go away because we as Americans have the capacity now, as we have had in the past, to do whatever needs to be done to preserve this last and greatest bastion of freedom.

In this present crisis, government is not the solution to our problem; government is the problem.

From time to time we have been tempted to believe that society has become too complex to be managed by self-rule, that government by an elite group is superior to government for, by, and of the people. But if no one among us is capable of governing himself, then who among us has the capacity to govern someone else?

All of us together—in and out of government—must bear the burden. The solutions we seek must be equitable with no one group singled out to pay a higher price. We hear much of special interest groups. Well, our concern must be for a special interest group that has been too long neglected.

It knows no sectional boundaries or ethnic and racial divisions, and it crosses political party lines. It is made up of men and women who raise our food, patrol our streets, man our mines and factories, teach our children, keep our homes, and heal us when we are sick—professionals, industrialists, shop keepers, clerks, cabbies, and truck drivers. They are, in short, "We the people," this breed called Americans.

Well, this Administration's objective will be a healthy vigorous, growing economy that provides equal opportunities for all Americans with no barriers born of bigotry or discrimination. Putting America back to work means putting all Americans back to work. Ending inflation means freeing all Americans from the terror of runaway living costs. All must share in the productive work of this "new beginning," and all must share in the bounty of a revived economy. With the idealism and fair play which are the core of our system and our strength, we can have a strong and prosperous America at peace with itself and the world.

So as we begin, let us take inventory. We are a nation that has a government—not the other way around. And this makes us special among the nations of the earth. Our government has no power except that granted it by the people. It is time to check and reverse the growth of government which shows signs of having grown beyond the consent of the governed.

It is my intention to curb the size and influence of the Federal establishment and to demand recognition of the distinction between the powers granted to the Federal government and those reserved to the states or to the people. (Applause.) All of us need to be reminded that the Federal government did not create the states; the states created the Federal government. (Applause.)

And so there will be no misunderstanding, it's not my intention to do away with government. It is rather to make it work—work with us, not over us; to stand by our side, not ride on our back. Government can and must provide opportunity, not smother it; foster productivity, not stifle it.

If we look for the answer as to why for so many years we achieved so much, prospered as no other people on earth, it was because here in this land we unleashed the energy and individual genius of man to a greater extent than has ever been done before. Freedom and the dignity of the individual have been more available and assured here than in any other place on earth. The price for this freedom at times has been high. But we have never been unwilling to pay that price.

It is no coincidence that our present troubles parallel and are proportionate to the intervention and intrusion in our lives that result from unnecessary and excessive growth of government.

It is time for us to realize that we are too great a nation to limit ourselves to small dreams. We're not, as some would have us believe, doomed to an inevitable decline. I do not believe in a fate that will fall on us no matter what we do. I do believe in a fate that will fall on us if we do nothing.

So with all the creative energy at our command, let us begin an era of national renewal. Let us renew our determination, our courage, and our strength. And let us renew our faith and our hope. We have every right to dream heroic dreams. Those who say that we're in a time when there are no heroes, they just don't know where to look. You can see heroes every day going in and out of factory gates. Others, a handful in number, produce enough food to feed all of us and then the world beyond.

You meet heroes across a counter. And they're on both sides of that counter. There are entrepreneurs with faith in themselves and faith in an idea who create new jobs, new wealth and opportunity. They're individuals and families whose taxes support the government and whose voluntary gifts support church, charity, culture, art, and education. Their patriotism is quiet but deep. Their values sustain our national life.

Now I have used the words "they" and "their" in speaking of these heroes. I could say "you" and "your" because I'm addressing the heroes of whom I speak—you, the citizens of this blessed land. Your dreams, your hopes, your goals are going to be the dreams, the hopes and the goals of this administration, so help me God. (Applause)

We shall reflect the compassion that is so much a part of your makeup. How can we love our country and not love our countrymen? And loving them reach out a hand when they fall, heal them when they're sick, and provide opportunity to make them self-sufficient so they will be equal in fact and not just in theory?

Can we solve the problems confronting us? Well, the answer is an unequivocal and emphatic yes. To paraphrase Winston Churchill, I did not take the oath I have just taken with the intention of presiding over the dissolution of the world's strongest economy.

In the days ahead I will propose removing the roadblocks that have slowed our economy and reduced productivity. Steps will be taken aimed at restoring the balance between the various levels of government. Progress may be slow, measured in inches and feet, not miles, but we will progress. It is time to reawaken this industrial giant, to get government back within its means, and to lighten our punitive tax burden, and these will be our first priorities, and on these principles there will be no compromise. (Applause.)

On the eve of our struggle for independence a man who might have been one of the greatest among the founding fathers, Dr. Joseph Warren, President of the Massachusetts Congress, said to his fellow Americans, "Our country is in danger, but not to be despaired of...On you depend the fortunes of America. You are to decide the important question upon which rests the happiness and the liberty of millions yet unborn. Act worthy of yourselves."

Well, I believe we, the Americans of today, are ready to act worthy of ourselves, ready to do what must be done to ensure happiness and liberty for ourselves, our children, and our children's children, and as we renew ourselves here in our own land we will be seen as having greater strength throughout the world. We will again be the exemplar of freedom and the beacon of hope for those who do not now have freedom.

To those neighbors and allies who share our freedom, we will strengthen our historic ties and assure them of our support and firm commitment. We will match loyalty with loyalty. We will strive for mutually beneficial relations. We will not use our friendship to impose on their sovereignty, for our own sovereignty is not for sale.

As for the enemies of freedom, those who are potential adversaries, they will be reminded that peace is the highest aspiration of the American people. We will negotiate for it, sacrifice for it; we will not surrender for it now or ever. (Applause.)

Our forbearance should never be misunderstood. Our reluctance for conflict should not be misjudged as a failure of will. When action is required to preserve our national security, we will act. We will maintain sufficient strength to prevail if need be, knowing that if we do so we have the best chance of never having to use that strength.

Above all we must realize that no arsenal or no weapon in the arsenals of the world is so formidable as the will and moral courage of free men and women. It is a weapon our adversaries in today's world do not have. It is a weapon that we as Americans do have. Let that be understood by those who practice terrorism and prey upon their neighbors. (Applause.)

I am told that tens of thousands of prayer meetings are being held on this day, and for that I'm deeply grateful. We are a nation under God, and I believe God intended for us to be free. It would be fitting and good, I think, if each Inaugural Day in future years should be declared a day of prayer.

This is the first time in our history that this ceremony has been held, as you have been told, on this West Front of the Capitol. Standing here, one faces a magnificent vista, opening up on this city's special beauty and history. At the end of this open mall are those shrines to the giants on whose shoulders we stand.

Directly in front of me, the monument to a monumental man, George Washington, Father of our country. A man of humility who came to greatness reluctantly. He led America out of revolutionary victory into infant nationhood.

Off to one side, the stately memorial to Thomas Jefferson. The Declaration of Independence flames with his eloquence.

And then beyond the reflecting pool, the dignified columns of the Lincoln Memorial. Whoever would understand in his heart the meaning of America will find it in the life of Abraham Lincoln.

Beyond those monuments to heroism is the Potomac River, and on the far shore the sloping hills of Arlington National Cemetery with its row upon row of simply white markers bearing crosses or Stars of David. They add up to only a tiny fraction of the price that has been paid for our freedom.

Each one of those markers is a monument to the kind of hero I spoke of earlier. Their lives ended in places called Belleau Wood, The Argonne, Omaha Beech, Salerno, and halfway around the world on Guadalcanal, Tarawa, Pork Chop Hill, the Chosin Reservoir, and in a hundred rice paddies and jungles of a place called Vietnam.

Under one such marker lies a young man—Martin Treptow —who left his job in a small town barber shop in 1917 to go to

France with the famed Rainbow Division. There, on the Western front, he was killed trying to carry a message between battalions under heavy artillery fire.

We are told that on his body was found a diary. On the flyleaf under the heading, "My Pledge," he had written these words: "America must win this war. Therefore I will work, I will save, I will sacrifice, I will endure, I will fight cheerfully and do my utmost, as if the issue of the whole struggle depended on me alone."

The crisis we are facing today does not require of us the kind of sacrifice that Martin Treptow and so many thousands of others were called upon to make. It does require, however, our best effort and our willingness to believe in ourselves and to believe in our capacity to perform great deeds, to believe that together with God's help we can and will resolve the problems which now confront us.

And after all, why shouldn't we believe that? We are Americans. God bless you and thank you. Thank you very much.

ADDRESS BY
THE PRESIDENT
TO A
JOINT SESSION OF CONGRESS
ON A PROGRAM FOR ECONOMIC RECOVERY

Perhaps the exact time history took a distinct turn in policy occurred at 11:42 A.M., January 20, 1981, when, with a resounding, "So Help me God!" Ronald Reagan pledged to uphold the constitution and became our fortieth President. He lost no time in trying to keep his campaign promise to turn America around. To do this Congress must accept his program for economic recovery. His triumphant speech to explain this plan before a joint session of Congress follows.

Only a month ago, I was your guest in this historic building and I pledged to you my cooperation in doing what is right for this Nation we all love so much.

I am here tonight to reaffirm that pledge and to ask that we share in restoring the promise that is offered to every citizen by this, the last, best hope of man on earth.

All of us are aware of the punishing inflation which has, for the first time in some 60 years, held to double digit figures for two years in a row. Interest rates have reached absurd levels of more than 20 percent and over 15 percent for those who would borrow to buy a home. All across this land one can see newly-built homes standing vacant, unsold because of mortgage interest rates.

Almost eight million Americans are out of work. These are people who want to be productive. But as the months go by, despair dominates their lives. The threats of layoff and unemployment hang over other millions, and all who work are frustrated by their inability to keep up with inflation.

One worker in a Midwest city put it to me this way: He said, "I'm bringing home more dollars than I thought I could ever earn but I seem to be getting worse off." Well, he is. Hourly earnings of the American worker, after adjusting for inflation, have declined five percent over the past five years. And furthermore, in the last five years, Federal personal taxes for the average family increased 67 percent.

We can no longer procrastinate and hope things will get better. They will not. If we do not act forcefully, and now, the economy will get worse.

Can we who man the ship of state deny it is out of control? Our national debt is approaching $1 trillion. A few weeks ago I called such a figure—a trillion dollars—incomprehensible. I've been trying to think of a way to illustrate how big it really is. The best I could come up with is to say that a stack of $1,000 bills in your hand only four inches high would make you a millionaire. A trillion dollars would be a stack of $1,000 bills 67 miles high.

The interest on the public debt this year will be over $90 billion. And unless we change the proposed spending for the fiscal year beginning October 1, we'll add another almost $80 billion to the debt.

Adding to our troubles is a mass of regulations imposed on the shopkeeper, the farmer, the craftsman, professionals and major industry that is estimated to add $100 billion to the price of things we buy and reduces our ability to produce.

The rate of increase in American productivity, once one of the highest in the world, is among the lowest of all major industrial nations. Indeed, it has actually declined the last three years.

I have painted a grim picture but I believe I have painted it accurately. It is within our power to change this picture and we can act in hope. There is nothing wrong with our internal strengths. There has been no breakdown in the human, technological, and natural resources upon which the economy is built.

Based on this confidence in a system which has never failed us—but which we have failed through a lack of confidence, and sometimes through a belief that we could fine tune the economy and get a tune more to our liking—I am proposing a comprehensive four-part program. I will now outline and give in some detail the principal parts of this program, but you will each be provided with a completely detailed copy of the program in its entirety.

This plan is aimed at reducing the growth in government spending and taxing, reforming and eliminating regulations which are unnecessary and counterproductive, and encouraging a consistent monetary policy aimed at maintaining the value of the currency.

If enacted in full, our program can help America create 13 million new jobs, nearly three million more than we would without these measures. It will also help us gain control of inflation.

It is important to note that we are only reducing the rate of increase in taxing and spending. We are not attempting to cut either spending or taxing to a level below that which we presently have. This plan will get our economy moving again, increase productivity growth, and thus create the jobs our people must have.

I am asking that you join me in reducing direct Federal spending by $41.4 billion in fiscal year 1982, along with $7.7 billion in user fees and off-budget savings for a total savings of $49.1 billion. This will still allow an increase of $40.8 billion over 1981 spending.

I know that exaggerated and inaccurate stories about these cuts have disturbed many people, particularly those dependent on grant and benefit programs for their basic needs. Some of you have heard from constituents afraid that Social Security checks, for example, might be taken from them. I regret the fear these unfounded stories have caused and welcome this opportunity to set things straight.

We will continue to fulfill the obligations that spring from our national conscience. Those who through no fault of their own must depend on the rest of us, the poverty stricken, the disabled, the elderly, all those with true need, can rest assured that the social safety net of programs they depend on are exempt from any cuts.

The full retirement benefits of the more than 31 million Social Security recipients will be continued along with an annual cost of living increase. Medicare will not be cut, nor will supplemental income for the blind, aged and disabled. Funding will continue for veterans' pensions.

School breakfasts and lunches for the children of low income families will continue as will nutrition and other special services for the aging. There will be no cut in Project Head Start or summer youth jobs.

All in all, nearly $216 billion providing help for tens of millions of Americans—will be fully funded. But government will not continue to subsidize individuals or particular business interests where real need cannot be demonstrated. And while we will reduce some subsidies to regional and local governments, we will at the same time convert a number of categorical grant programs into block grants to reduce wasteful administrative overhead and to give local government entities and States more flexibility and control. We call for an end to duplication in Federal programs and reform of those which are not cost effective.

Already, some have protested there must be no reduction of aid to schools. Let me point out that Federal aid to education amounts to only eight percent of total educational funding. For this the Federal Government has insisted on a tremendously disproportionate share of control over our schools. Whatever reductions we've proposed in that eight percent will amount to very little of the total cost of education. It will, however, restore more authority to States and local school districts.

Historically the American people have supported by voluntary contributions more artistic and cultural activities than all the other countries in the world put together. I wholeheartedly support this approach and believe Americans will continue their generosity. Therefore, I am proposing a savings of $85 million in the Federal subsidies now going to the arts and humanities.

There are a number of subsidies to business and industry I believe are unnecessary. Not because the activities being subsidized aren't of value but because the marketplace contains incentives enough to warrant continuing these activities without a government subsidy. One such subsidy is the Department of Energy's synthetic fuels program. We will continue support of research leading to development of new technologies and more independence from foreign oil, but we can save at least $3.2 billion by leaving to private industry the building of plants to make liquid or gas fuels from coal.

We are asking that another major business subsidy, the Export-Import Bank loan authority, be reduced by one-third in 1982. We are doing this because the primary beneficiaries of taxpayer funds in this case are the exporting companies themselves—most of them profitable corporations.

And this brings me to a number of other lending programs in which government makes low-interest loans, some of them for an interest rate as low as 2 percent. What has not been very well understood is that the Treasury Department has no money of its own. It has to go into the private capital market and borrow the money to provide those loans. In this time of excessive interest rates the government finds itself paying interest several times as high as it receives from the borrowing agency. The taxpayers—your constituents—of course, are paying that high interest rate and it just makes all other interest rates higher.

By terminating the Economic Development Administration we can save hundreds of millions of dollars in 1982 and billions more over the next few years. There is a lack of consistent and convincing evidence that E.D.A. and its Regional Commissions have been effective in creating new jobs. They have been effective in creating an array of planners, grantsmen and professional middlemen. We believe we can do better just by the expansion of the economy and the job creation which will come from our economic program.

The Food Stamp program will be restored to its original purpose, to assist those without resources to purchase sufficient nutritional food. We will, however, save $1.8 billion in FY 1982 by removing from eligibility those who are not in real need or who are abusing the program. Despite this reduction, the program will be budgeted for more than $10 billion.

We will tighten welfare and give more attention to outside sources of income when determining the amount of welfare an individual is allowed. This plus strong and effective work requirements will save $520 million next year.

I stated a moment ago our intention to keep the school breakfast and lunch programs for those in true need. But by cutting back on meals for children of families who can afford to pay, the savings will be $1.6 billion in FY 1982.

Let me just touch on a few other areas which are typical of the kind of reductions we have included in this economic package. The Trade Adjustment Assistance program provides benefits for workers who are unemployed when foreign imports reduce the market for various American products causing shutdown of plants and layoff of workers. The purpose is to help these workers find jobs in growing sectors of our economy. And yet, because these benefits are paid out on top of normal unemployment benefits, we wind up paying greater benefits to those who lose their jobs because of foreign competition than we do to their friends and neighbors who are laid off due to domestic competition. Anyone must agree that this is unfair. Putting these two programs on the same footing will save $1.15 billion in just one year.

Earlier I made mention of changing categorical grants to States and local governments into block grants. We know of course that categorical grant programs burden local and State governments with a mass of Federal regulations and Federal paperwork.

Ineffective targeting, wasteful administrative overhead—all can be eliminated by shifting the resources and decision-making authority to local and State government. This will also consolidate programs which are scattered throughout the Federal bureaucracy. It will bring government closer to the people and will save $23.9 billion over the next five years.

Our program for economic renewal deals with a number of programs which at present are not cost-effective. An example is Medicaid. Right now Washington provides the States with unlimited matching payments for their expenditures. At the same time we here in Washington pretty much dictate how the States will manage the program. We want to put a cap on how much the Federal Government will contribute but at the same time allow the States much more flexibility in managing and structuring their programs. I know from our experience in California that such flexibility could have led to far more cost-effective reforms. This will bring a savings of $1 billion next year.

The space program has been and is important to America and we plan to continue it. We believe, however, that a re-ordering of priorities to focus on the most important and cost-effective NASA programs can result in a savings of a quarter of a billion dollars.

Coming down from space to the mailbox—the Postal Service has been consistently unable to live within its operating budget. It is still dependent on large Federal subsidies. We propose reducing those subsidies by $632 million in 1982 to press the Postal Service into becoming more effective. In subsequent years, the savings will continue to add up.

The Economic Regulatory Administration in the Department of Energy has programs to force companies to convert

44

to specific fuels. It has the authority to administer a gas rationing plan, and prior to decontrol it ran the oil price control program. With these and other regulations gone we can save several hundreds of millions of dollars over the next few years.

Now I'm sure there is one department you've been waiting for me to mention. That is the Department of Defense. It is the only department in our entire program that will actually be increased over the present budgeted figure. But even here there was no exemption. The Department of Defense came up with a number of cuts which reduced the budget increase needed to restore our military balance. These measures will save $2.9 billion in 1982 outlays and by 1986 a total of $28.2 billion will have been saved. The aim will be to provide the most effective defense for the lowest possible cost.

I believe my duty as President requires that I recommend increases in defense spending over the coming years. Since 1970 the Soviet Union has invested $300 billion more in its military forces than we have. As a result of its massive military buildup, the Soviets now have a significant numerical advantage in strategic nuclear delivery systems, tactical aircraft, submarines, artillery and anti-aircraft defense. To allow this imbalance to continue is a threat to our national security.

Notwithstanding our economic straits, making the financial changes beginning now is far less costly than waiting and attempting a crash program several years from now.

We remain committed to the goal of arms limitation through negotiation and hope we can persuade our adversaries to come to realistic balanced and verifiable agreements. But, as we negotiate, our security must be fully protected by a balanced and realistic defense program.

Let me say a word here about the general problem of waste

and fraud in the Federal Government. One government estimate indicated that fraud alone may account for anywhere from 1 to 10 percent — as much as $25 billion — of Federal expenditures for social programs. If the tax dollars that are wasted or mismanaged are added to this fraud total, the staggering dimensions of this problem begin to emerge.

The Office of Management and Budget is now putting together an interagency task force to attack waste and fraud. We are also planning to appoint as Inspectors General highly-trained professionals who will spare no effort to do this job.

No administration can promise to immediately stop a trend that has grown in recent years as quickly as Government expenditures themselves. But let me say this: waste and fraud in the Federal budget is exactly what I have called it before—an unrelenting national scandal—a scandal we are bound and determined to do something about.

Marching in lockstep with the whole program of reductions in spending is the equally important program of reduced tax rates. Both are essential if we are to have economic recovery. It is time to create new jobs, build and rebuild industry, and give the American people room to do what they do best. And that can only be done with a tax program which provides incentive to increase productivity for both workers and industry.

Our proposal is for a 10-percent across-the-board cut every year for three years in the tax rates for all individual income taxpayers making a total tax cut of 30 percent. This three-year reduction will also apply to the tax on unearned income leading toward an eventual elimination of the present differential between the tax on earned and unearned income.

The effective starting date for these 10 percent personal

income tax rate reductions will be July 1st of this year.

Again, let me remind you this 30 percent reduction in marginal rates, while it will leave the taxpayers with $500 billion more in their pockets over the next five years, is actually only a reduction in the tax increase already built into the system.

Unlike some past tax "reforms," this is not merely a shift of wealth between different sets of taxpayers. This proposal for an equal reduction in everyone's tax rates will expand our national prosperity, enlarge national incomes, and increase opportunities for all Americans.

Some will argue, I know, that reducing tax rates now will be inflationary. A solid body of economic experts does not agree. And certainly tax cuts adopted over the past three-fourths of a century indicate these economic experts are right. The advice I have had is that by 1985 our real production of goods and services will grow by 20 percent and will be $300 billion higher than it is today. The average worker's wage will rise (in real purchasing power) by eight percent and those are after-tax dollars. This, of course, is predicated on our complete program of tax cuts and spending reductions being implemented.

The other part of the tax package is aimed directly at providing business and industry with the capital needed to modernize and engage in more research and development. This will involve an increase in depreciation allowances and this part of our tax proposal will be retroactive to January 1st.

The present depreciation system is obsolete, needlessly complex, and economically counterproductive. Very simply, it bases the depreciation of plant, machinery, vehicles, and tools on their original cost with no recognition of how inflation has increased their replacement cost. We are proposing a much shorter write-off time than is presently allowed. We propose a five-year write-off for machinery; three years for vehicles and trucks; and a ten-year write-off for plants.

In Fiscal Year 1982 under this plan business would acquire nearly $10 billion for investment and by 1985 the figure would be nearly $45 billion. These changes are essential to provide the new investment which is needed to create millions of new jobs between now and 1986 and to make America competitive once again in world markets. These are not make-work jobs, they are productive jobs with a future.

I'm well aware that there are many other desirable tax changes such as indexing the income tax brackets to protect taxpayers against inflation. There is the unjust discrimination against married couples if both are working and earning, tuition tax credits, the unfairness of the inheritance tax especially to the family-owned farm and the family-owned business and a number of others. But our program for economic recovery is so urgently needed to begin to bring down inflation that I would ask you to act on this plan first and with great urgency. Then I pledge to you I will join with you in seeking these additional tax changes at an early date.

American society experienced a virtual explosion in Government regulation during the past decades. Between 1970 and 1979, expenditures for the major regulatory agencies quadrupled, the number of pages published annually in the *Federal Register* nearly tripled, and the number of pages in the *Code of Federal Regulations* increased by nearly two-thirds.

The result has been higher prices, higher unemployment, and lower productivity growth. Overregulation causes small and independent businessmen and women, as well as large businesses, to defer or terminate plans for expansion and, since they are responsible for most of our new jobs, those new jobs aren't created.

We have no intention of dismantling the regulatory agencies—especially those necessary to protect the environment and to assure the public health and safety. However, we must come to grips with inefficient and burdensome regulations—eliminate those we can and reform those we must keep.

I have asked Vice President Bush to head a Cabinet-level Task Force on Regulatory Relief. Second, I asked each member of my Cabinet to postpone the effective dates of the hundreds of regulations which have not yet been implemented. Third, in coordination with the Task Force, many of the agency heads have taken prompt action to review and rescind existing burdensome regulations. Finally, just yesterday, I signed an Executive Order that for the first time provides for effective and coordinated management of the regulatory process.

Although much has been accomplished, this is only a beginning. We will eliminate those regulations that are unproductive and unnecessary by Executive Order where possible and cooperate fully with you on those that require legislation.

The final aspect of our plan requires a national monetary policy which does not allow money growth to increase consistently faster than the growth of goods and services. In order to curb inflation, we need to slow the growth in our money supply.

We fully recognize the independence of the Federal Reserve System and will do nothing to undermine that independence. We will consult regularly with the Federal Reserve Board on all aspects of our economic program and will vigorously pursue budget policies that will make their job easier in reducing monetary growth.

A successful program to achieve stable and moderate growth patterns in the money supply will keep both inflation and interest rates down and restore vigor to our financial institutions and markets.

This, then, is our proposal. "America's New Beginning: A Program for Economic Recovery." I do not want it to be simply the plan of my Administration—I am here tonight to ask you to join me in making it our plan. Together, we can embark on this road not to make things easy, but to make things better.

Can we do the job? The answer is yes. But we must begin now. Our social, political and cultural, as well as our economic institutions, can no longer absorb the repeated shocks that have been dealt them over the past decades.

We are in control here. There is nothing wrong with America that we can't fix. So I'm full of hope and optimism that we will see this difficult new challenge to its end — that we will find those reservoirs of national will to once again do the right thing.

I'm sure there will be some who will raise the familiar old cry, "don't touch my program—cut somewhere else."

I hope I've made it plain that our approach has been even-handed; that only the programs for the truly deserving needy remain untouched.

The question is, are we simply going to go down the same path we've gone down before—carving out one special program here and another special program there. I don't think that is what the American people expect of us. More important, I don't think that is what they want. They are ready to return to the source of our strength.

The substance and prosperity of our Nation is built by wages brought home from the factories and the mills, the farms and the ships. They are the services provided in 10,000 corners of America; the interest on the thrift of our people and the returns from their risk-taking. The production of America is the possession of those who build, serve, create and produce.

For too long now, we've removed from our people the decisions on how to dispose of what they created. We have strayed from first principles. We must alter our course.

The taxing power of government must be used to provide revenues for legitimate government purposes. It must not be used to regulate the economy or bring about social change. We've tried that and surely must be able to see it doesn't work.

Spending by Government must be limited to those functions which are the proper province of Government. We can no longer afford things simply because we think of them.

Next year we can reduce the budget by $41.4 billion, without harm to Government's legitimate purposes and to our responsibility to all who need our benevolence. This, plus the reduction in tax rates, will help bring an end to inflation.

In the health and social services area alone the plan we are proposing will substantially reduce the need for 465 pages of law, 1400 pages of regulations and 5000 Federal employees who presently administer 7,600 separate grants at about 25,000 locations. Over 7 million man and woman hours of work by state and local officials are required to fill our Federal forms.

May I direct a question to those who have indicated unwillingness to accept this plan for a new beginning: an economic recovery? Have they an alternative which offers a greater chance of balancing the budget, reducing and eliminating inflation, stimulating the creation of jobs, and reducing the tax burden? And, if they haven't, are they suggesting we can continue on the present course without coming to a day of reckoning in the very near future?

If we don't do this, inflation and a growing tax burden will put an end to everything we believe in and to our dreams for the future. We do not have an option of living with inflation and its attendant tragedy, of millions of productive people willing and able to work but unable to find buyers in the job market.

We have an alternative to that, a program for economic recovery, a program that will balance the budget, put us well on the road to our ultimate objective of eliminating inflation entirely, increasing productivity and creating millions of new jobs.

True, it will take time for the favorable effects of our proposal to be felt. So we must begin now.

The people are watching and waiting. They don't demand miracles, but they do expect us to act. Let us act together.

Thank you and good night.

ADDRESS BY
PRESIDENT RONALD REAGAN
TO A
JOINT SESSION OF CONGRESS
APRIL 28, 1981

If there were any Americans who still doubted Ronald Reagan was "for real," those doubts ended as the shots of a would-be assassin's gun rang out. "The President is shot," cried a crowd of people who witnessed the shooting! President Reagan was rushed to surgery, and though near death, fought valiantly for his life. So miraculous was his recovery, he held meetings in his hospital suite, so that his economic program would not lose momentum.

Only three weeks after the tragic shooting, he was back to Capitol Hill delivering another address to a joint session of Congress. This speech received four standing ovations. So great was its impact that it convinced Congress to vote overwhelmingly in favor of his plan.

A new American hero was born.

Mr. Speaker, Mr. President, distinguished members of the Congress, honored guests, and fellow citizens, I have no words to express my appreciation for that greeting.

I have come to speak to you tonight about our economic recovery program, and why I believe it's essential that the Congress approve this package, which I believe will lift the crushing burden of inflation off our citizens and restore the vitality to our economy and our industrial machine.

First, however, and due to events of the past few weeks, will you permit me to digress for a moment from the all-important subject of why we must bring government spending under control and reduce tax rates.

I'd like to say a few words directly to all of you and to those who are watching and listening tonight, because this is the only way I know to express to all of you on behalf of Nancy and myself our appreciation for your messages, your flowers, and most of all, your prayers, not only for me but for those others who fell beside me. The warmth of your words, the expression of friendship, and yes love, meant more to us than you can ever know. You have given us a memory that we will treasure forever. And you have provided an answer to those few voices that were raised saying that what happened was evidence that ours is a sick society.

The society we heard from is made up of millions of compassionate Americans and their children from college age to kindergarten. As a matter of fact as evidence of that, I have a letter with me. The letter came from Peter Sweeney. He's in the second grade in the Riverside school in Rockville Center, and he said, "I hope you get well quick or you might have to make a speech in your pajamas." He added a post script, "P.S., if you have to make a speech in your pajamas, I warned you." Well, sick societies don't produce men like the two who recently returned from outer space. Sick societies don't produce young men like Secret Service Agent Tim McCarthy, who placed his body between mine and the man with the gun simply because he felt that's what his duty called for him to do. Sick societies don't produce dedicated police officers like Tom Delahanty, or able and devoted public servants like Jim Brady. Sick societies don't make people like us so proud to be Americans and so very proud of our fellow citizens.

Now, let's talk about getting spending and inflation under control and cutting your tax rates. Mr. Speaker and Senator Baker, I want to thank you for your cooperation in helping to arrange this joint session of the Congress. I won't be speaking to you very long tonight, but I asked for this meeting because the urgency of our joint mission is not changed. Thanks to some very fine people my health is much improved. I'd like to be able to say *that* with regard to the health of the economy. It's been half a year since the election that charged all of us in government the task of restoring the economy. Where have we come in these six months? Inflation is measured by the Consumer Price Index and has continued at a double digit rate. Mortgage interest rates have averaged almost 15% for these six months, preventing families across America from buying homes. There are still almost eight million unemployed. The average worker's hourly earnings after adjusting for inflation are lower today than they were six months ago, and there have been over six thousand business failures. Six months is long enough. The American people now want us to act and not in half measures. They demand and they have earned a full and comprehensive effort to clean up our economic mess. Because of the extent of our economy's sickness we know that the cure will not come quickly and that even with our package, progress will come in inches and feet not in miles. But to fail to act will delay even longer and more painfully the cure which must come, and that cure begins with the Federal budget. And the budgetary actions taken by the Congress over the next few days will determine how we respond to the message of last November 4. That message was very simple —our government is too big and it spends too much.

The last few months you and I have enjoyed a relationship

based on extraordinary cooperation. Because of this cooperation we've come a long distance in less than three months. I want to thank the leadership of the Congress for helping in setting a fair timetable for consideration of our recommendations. And committee chairmen on both sides of the aisle have called prompt and fair hearings. We have also communicated in a spirit of candor, openness, and mutual respect. Tonight, as our decision day nears, and as the House of Representatives weighs its alternatives, I wish to address you in that same spirit.

The Senate Budget Committee, under the leadership of Pete Domenici, has just today voted out a budget resolution supported by Democrats and Republicans alike, that is in all major respects consistent with the program that we have proposed. Now we look forward to favorable action on the Senate floor, but an equally crucial test involves the House of Representatives. The House will soon be choosing between two different versions or measures to deal with the economy. One is the measure offered by the House Budget Committee, the other is a bipartisan measure, a substitute introduced by Congressman Phil Gramm of Texas and Del Latta of Ohio. On behalf of the administration let me say that we embrace and fully support that bipartisan substitute. It will achieve all the essential aims of controlling government spending, reducing the tax burden, building a national defense second to none, and stimulating economic growth and creating millions of new jobs. At the same time, however, I must state our opposition to the measure offered by the House Budget Committee.

It may appear that we have two alternatives. In reality, however, there are no more alternatives left. The committee measure quite simply falls far too short of the essential actions that we must take. For example, in the next three years the committee measure projects spending one hundred forty billion dollars more than does the bipartisan substitute. It regrettably cuts over fourteen billion dollars in essential defense spending funding required to restore America's national security. It adheres to the failed policy of trying to balance the budget on the taxpayers back. It would increase tax payments by over a third, adding up to a staggering quarter of a trillion dollars. Federal taxes would increase 12% each year. Taxpayers would be paying a larger share of their income to government in 1984 than they do at present. In short, that measure reflects an echo of the past rather than a benchmark for the future. High taxes and excess spending growth created our present economic mess. More of the same will not cure the hardship, anxiety and discouragement it has imposed on the American people.

Let us cut through the fog for a moment. The answer to a government that's too big is to stop feeding its growth. Government spending has been growing faster than the economy itself. The massive national debt which we accumulated is the result of the government's high spending diet. Well, it's time to change the diet and to change it in the right way. I know the tax portion of our package is of concern to some of you, but let me make a few points that I feel have been overlooked. First of all it should be looked at as an integral part of the entire package, not something separate and apart from the budget reductions, the regulatory relief, and the monetary restraints. Probably the most common misconception is that we are proposing to reduce government revenues to less than what the government has been receiving. This is not true.

Actually, the discussion has to do with how much of a tax increase should be imposed on the taxpayer in 1982. Now I know that over the recess in some informal polling some of your constituents have been asked which they would rather have, a balanced budget or a tax cut, and with the common sense that characterizes the people of this country, the answer, of course, has been a balanced budget. But, may I suggest, with no inference that there was wrong intent on the part of those who asked the question, the question was inappropriate to the situation. Our choice is not between a balanced budget and a tax cut. Properly asked, the question is, do you want a great big raise in your taxes this coming year, or at the worst, a very little increase with the prospect of tax reduction and a balanced budget down the road a ways? With the common sense that the people have already shown, I am sure we all know what the answer to that question would be.

A gigantic tax increase has been built into the system. We propose nothing more than a reduction of that increase. The people have a right to know that even with our plan they will be paying more in taxes but not as much more as they will without it. The option, I believe, offered by the House Budget Committee will leave spending too high and tax rates too high. At the same time I think it cuts the defense budget too much. And by attempting to reduce the deficit through higher taxes it will not create the kind of strong economic growth and the new jobs that we must have. Let us not overlook the fact that the small independent businessman or woman creates more than 80% of all the new jobs and employs more than half of our total work force. Our across-the-board cut in tax rates for a three year period will give them much of the incentive and promise of stability they need to go forward with expansion

58

plans calling for additional employees.

Tonight I renew my call for us to work as a team, to join in cooperation so that we find answers which will begin to solve all our economic problems and not just some of them. The economic recovery package that I have outlined to you over the past few weeks is, I deeply believe, the only answer that we have left. Reducing the growth of spending, cutting marginal tax rates, providing relief from over-regulation, and following a non-inflationary and predictable monetary policy, are interwoven measures which will insure that we have addressed each of the severe dislocations which threaten our economic future. These policies will make our economy stronger, and the stronger economy will balance the budget which we are committed to do by 1984.

When I took the oath of office I pledged loyalty to only one special interest group—we the people. Those people, neighbors and friends, shopkeepers and laborers, farmers and craftsmen, do not have infinite patience. As a matter of fact, some eighty years ago Teddy Roosevelt wrote these instructive words in his first message to the Congress, "the American people are slow to wrath, but when their wrath is once kindled it burns like a consuming flame." Well, perhaps that kind of wrath will be deserved if our answer to these serious problems is to repeat the mistakes of the past. The old and comfortable way is to shave a little here and add a little there. Well, that's not acceptable any more. I think this great and historic Congress knows that way is no longer acceptable. I think you have shown that you know the one sure way to continue the inflationary spiral is to fall back into the predictable patterns of old economic practices. Isn't it time that we tried something new? When you allowed me to speak to you here in these chambers a little earlier, I told you that I wanted this program for economic recovery to be ours—yours and mine. I think the bipartisan substitute bill has achieved that purpose. It moves us toward an economic vitality.

Just two weeks ago you and I joined millions of our fellow Americans in marveling at the magic historical moment that John Young and Bob Crippen created in their space shuttle, Columbia. The last manned effort was almost six years ago, and I remembered on this more recent day over the years how we had all come to expect technological precision of our men and machines, and each amazing achievement became commonplace until the next new challenge was raised. With the space shuttle we tested our ingenuity once again, moving beyond the accomplishments of the past into the promise and uncertainty of the future. Thus, we not only planned to send up a 122 foot aircraft, 170 miles into space, but we also intended to make it maneuverable and return it to earth landing 98 tons of exotic metals delicately on a remote dry lake bed. The space shuttle did more than prove our technological abilities. It raised our expectations once more. It started us dreaming again. The poet Carl Sandberg wrote, "The republic is a dream; nothing happens unless first a dream". And that's what makes us as Americans different.

We've always reached for a new spirit and aimed at a higher goal. We have been courageous and determined, unafraid and bold. Who among us wants to be first to say we no longer have those qualities, that we must limp along doing the same things that have brought us our present misery. I believe that the people you and I represent are ready to chart a new course. They look to us to meet the great challenge, to reach beyond the commonplace and not fall short for lack of creativity or courage. Someone once said, "he who would have nothing to do with thorns, must never attempt to gather flowers." Well, we have much greatness before us. We can restore our economic strength and build opportunities like none we have ever had before. As Carl Sandberg said, "All we need to begin with is a dream and we can do better than before." All we need to have is faith and that dream will come true. All we need to do is act, and the time for action is now. Thank you.

Overleaf: *State of the Union address—February, 1981 to a combined session of Congress.*

Photo/Dirck Halstead—*Time*